Hydrochloric acid – This is another strong acid and is found in your stomach, where it breaks down foods to allow them to be digested.

Nitric acid – A strong acid, formed when nitrogen dioxide is dissolved in water.

Ethanoic acid – This is the main ingredient in vinegar. It is a weak acid and, not surprisingly, smells strongly of vinegar!

Ammonia – This is a gas that dissolves in water to form a weak alkali. It is found in many household bleaches and cleaning products.

Sodium bicarbonate (sodium hydrogen carbonate) – Also known as baking soda, this is another weak alkali. It reacts with acids to give off carbon dioxide.

Sodium hydroxide – This is a very strong alkali, also called caustic soda. It can be used (with great care!) for clearing outside drains but is mainly used in industry for removing unwanted acids.

When was the pH scale invented?

It was first introduced in 1909 by a Danish chemist named Søren Peder Lauritz Sørensen (1868–1939).

How long have we known about acid rain?

Acid rain was first reported in the 1850s by Robert Angus Smith, a Scottish chemist working in Manchester (England). Smith first used the term 'acid rain' in 1872.

Acid rain

Acid rain is produced when acidic gases (such as sulphur dioxide and nitrogen oxide) enter the atmosphere. These gases react with the oxygen and water vapour in the atmosphere to form dilute solutions of sulphuric and nitric acids. When this acidic solution falls as rainwater it can cause serious damage to plants and animal life as well as corroding stone buildings and monuments. Fish and other aquatic life can be particularly badly affected – besides falling directly into the water they live in, acid rain falling over a wide area will naturally be channelled into rivers, lakes and streams! The principal cause of acid rain is acknowledged to be the pollutants given off from industrial processes, particularly the burning of fossil fuels like oil and coal in power stations. These fuels contain sulphur and will produce sulphur dioxide when burned.

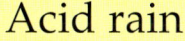
fascinating facts

Many species of fish cannot survive if their environment falls below a pH of about 4.2.

As you move down the pH scale from 14, each level is 10 times more acidic than the one before – so a concentrated solution of a strong acid (pH 0) is 10 million times more acidic than water!

Darwin *and* evolution

Charles Darwin (1809-82) was one of England's most famous scientists. His studies of plants and animals lead to his famous theories about a process called 'evolution'. Evolution is the idea that plants and animals have changed, developed or 'evolved' over time. Many 19th century scientists who studied living animals and the fossils of extinct ones were interested in evolution. A fossil is an animal or plant that has been preserved for millions of years. Darwin was one of the first people to suggest how evolution might happen and to make society take notice of these ideas.

Voyage around the world

As a young boy, Darwin was very interested in nature and the world around him. He went on long hikes and helped his older brother with his chemistry experiments. While at Cambridge University he was introduced to the Rev. John Stevens Henslow who was a professor of botany (the science or study of plants). Henslow got Darwin a job as a naturalist (somebody who is knowledgeable about natural history) on the HMS Beagle in 1831. The ship sailed on a five-year round-the-world voyage in order to study the coasts of South America, Australia, New Zealand and many smaller islands.

On the voyage, Darwin collected evidence of many new species (types) of plants and animals. He also began to think about evolution after he found lots of different species of tortoises on different islands. He had a theory that all the different tortoises had originated (come from) a single species of tortoise and had adapted to life in different ways, eventually becoming many different species.

Creation

In the Biblical account of creation, the earth was created by God in seven days and humans and all the animals were created in the forms we know today. Evolution argued that

Does everyone believe in evolution?

Although the scientific theory of evolution has been accepted by most people today, some still believe in the literal truth of the Bible.

Were Darwin and Wallace the first people to think about evolution?

No. An ancient Greek philosopher (thinker) called Aristotle believed that 'higher' forms of life had descended or 'evolved' from 'lower' forms.

this was not the case, and that animals developed gradually over many millions of years.

On the Origin of Species by means of Natural Selection

In 1858 a young scientist called A. R. Wallace sent Darwin an essay he had written. Darwin was shocked to find Wallace had the same ideas as his own! The two men decided to publish their ideas at the same time, announcing them at a joint lecture. Darwin rushed to finish his book and published it in 1859. It was called 'On the Origin of Species by means of Natural Selection' , normally shortened to On the Origin of Species.

Darwin's theory of natural selection argues that species that are better adapted to their environment will reproduce more readily than those that are not well adapted. Over time, characteristics that are advantageous, such as resistance to disease and the ability to find food, will be passed on through the generations, whereas characteristics that are disadvantageous, such as susceptibility to disease, will die out. This process may result in new species developing, which may be more complex than their predecessors. For example, there is a theory that apes and humans had the same ancestors, just as the different species of tortoise found by Darwin had the same common ancestor but had adapted in different ways.

The way natural selection works can be seen in 'selective breeding'. This is when people breed plants and animals in order to encourage certain characteristics, for example, making larger hens or brighter flowers. For example, the vegetables cabbage, kale, Brussel sprouts and cauliflower were all bred from the same wild plant!

Darwin continued to work on his theories until he died. The importance of all his work was recognised and he was given a state funeral. He was buried in Westminster Abbey, near other famous scientists like Isaac Newton.

Before Darwin, people thought that species had never changed throughout history.

fascinaTing FacT

Einstein

Albert Einstein (1879–1955) is considered one of the most important scientists of the 20th century. His name has become another word for genius, so if you say that someone is an Einstein, you are saying that person is extremely intelligent.

Einstein's childhood

Einstein spent his childhood in Germany. His father showed him a compass when he was five, and he realised that some kind of force must have been moving the needle. This was one of the most important moments in Einstein's life. Although he was thought to be a slow learner, he was very good at mathematics at school, and also built models and mechanical toys for fun. Having studied his brain after death, scientists now think he learned differently from other people because of the way his brain was made up.

The Special Theory of Relativity

After he left school he got a job working in the Swiss patent office. He spent all of his spare time studying physics. Whilst there, he came up with his Special Theory of Relativity (1905) and studied the movement of atoms. Einstein assumed that everything in the universe was moving and so all motion and all measurements we take are relative. However, Einstein's theory says that the speed of light is constant and that nothing can move faster than light. Time and space are normally thought of as different, separate things. Einstein thought of them as one thing, and that they acted together. Instead of talking about things having three co-ordinates (three dimensions in space), he gave them four co-ordinates (the fourth being time). It is from Einstein that science fiction gets the term 'space-time continuum'! Einstein's Special Theory abandoned the traditional laws of physics and geometry.

The General Theory of Relativity

Albert Einstein became Dr Albert Einstein and worked at many universities as a professor. In his General Theory of Relativity (1915), he pointed out that light rays passing near the sun must be bent very slightly by the sun's gravitational pull. Eclipse observers in 1919 and 1922 proved that this was true, and he became world famous.

In his theory, Einstein argued that objects become heavier when they move faster, and so people can never travel at the speed of light because they would become vastly (perhaps even infinitely) heavy. Einstein's theories are most important in astronomy and when studying atomic particles that travel at vast speeds.

The Einstein Cross

In 1936 Einstein wrote about gravitational lensing, which means the light from a distant source appears to be spaced around another bright object which is not so distant. This became known as the Einstein Cross (right). The central light spot is about 400 million light years away, while the outer light spots are 8 billion light years away!

Q&A?

E=mc² Einstein's most famous equation. But what does it mean?

It means that the energy of a body at rest (E) equals its mass (m) multiplied by the speed of light (c) squared.

Why didn't Einstein wear socks?

He hated the way that the big toe makes a hole in a sock, so he stopped wearing them.

Highest honours

Einstein was awarded the Nobel Prize for Physics in 1921 for general contributions to the study of physics. At this point, some fellow scientists still disagreed with him about his theories on relativity.

Later work

In 1934, Einstein's possessions and his German citizenship were taken away from him by the German Nazi government because he was Jewish. He had already accepted a job in the United States, so he left Germany. In the United States he worked on a wider extension of his theories, publishing his Unified Field Theory in 1950. This theory expanded his earlier theories to include his ideas about electricity and magnetism, explaining both these forces. But Einstein never found a way to test it.

Fascinating Facts

Einstein was very forgetful.

As a child, Einstein was given violin lessons. He hated them, and gave up the instrument, but later, he enjoyed listening to Mozart's violin works.

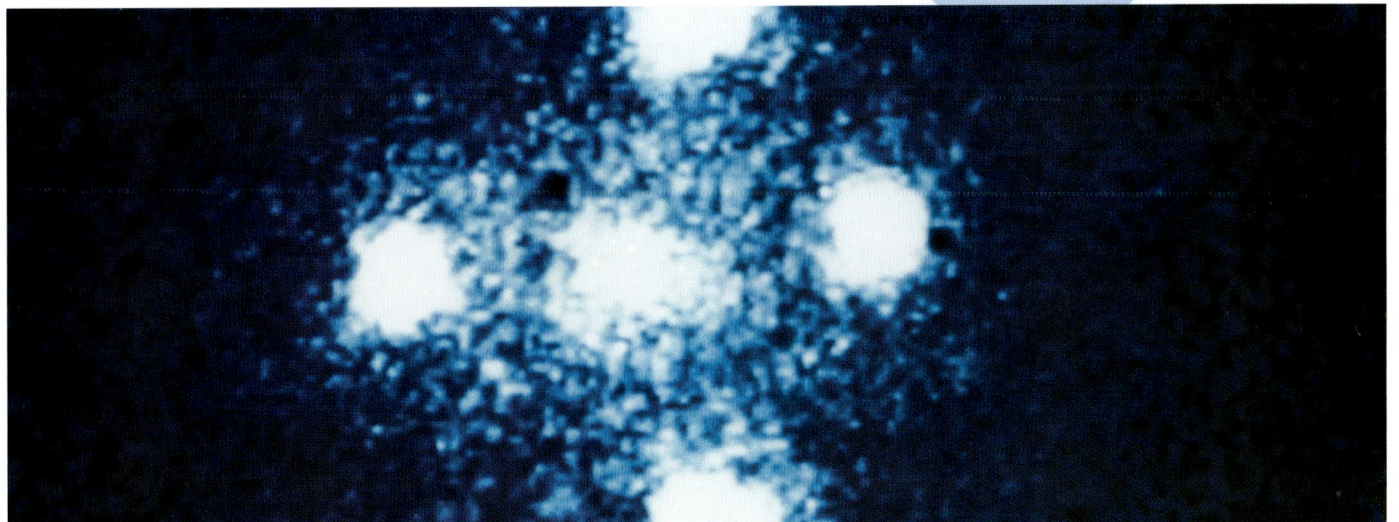

Energy *natural and* manufactured

Energy is what makes us grow and move. It is also heat, light, and sound. Plants store energy, and as they grow they obtain energy from the soil and light energy from the sun. This process is called photosynthesis.

Humans and animals get their energy from the nutrients and calories in food and drink. When you eat, your body uses food as fuel. Even when you think, you are using energy your body has gained from food you've eaten.

There are different kinds of energy. If you ride a bicycle, your body provides the energy to move the pedals and wheels. When a car moves, its energy comes from the fuel in its engine. We use energy to heat houses, power cars and buses, and for radios and factory machines. The technology we use in modern life requires a lot of energy.

Power station

Q&A?

What happens if a television is left on standby?

A television or stereo left on standby will use between 10% and 60% of the energy it would use if it were switched on.

How can I save energy?

Turn off lights when you leave a room, use energy-saving light bulbs, and never overfill the kettle.

A computer monitor left on overnight wastes the amount of energy it would take to print 800 pages.

Most of the power we use every day is from electrical energy. Electricity is very convenient as it can be easily carried by wires (above) to the electric sockets in our houses or stored in batteries. Most electricity is generated at power stations.

Power stations

Most power stations use fossil fuels such as coal, oil, and gas. The fuel is burned to heat water, which turns into steam, and the steam is used to move the parts of the generator, which produces electricity. Steam power was used to power trains in the early days of the railways.

Oil is also used to make the petrol that powers all our cars and buses. Fossil fuels are a finite resource: there is a limited supply of them, and we will eventually use them up. Many people ask what alternative energy sources we can use when the fossil fuels run out.

Hydroelectric power

Hydroelectric power is produced when the moving energy of falling water at river dams is used to power electric generators. The traditional version of this was the water wheel, used in small rivers and streams to power grain mills and early factories. Hydroelectric power can also be obtained from tidal energy using the twice-daily movement of the sea's tides.

Solar power

Solar power is produced when the energy from the sun is turned into electricity. Some people have solar panels (right) on the roofs of their houses to provide the power to heat the water for their baths or power their light bulbs. Solar

power plants are possible in very sunny parts of the world, but a wide area of ground would have to be covered by solar panels to provide sufficient electricity.

Wind power

Wind power is produced when turbines harness the power of the wind, especially in coastal areas where winds are strongest. Windmills have been used for hundreds of years as a source of power, but with modern technologies wind power can now be collected on a large scale from wind farms (below). Wind power is converted into electricity.

Nuclear power

Nuclear power is produced when a controlled nuclear reaction is used to power a large generator. Nuclear power stations create large amounts of energy, but the fuels they use are rare and expensive, and people worry that they are not safe and that they are harmful to the planet. There have been accidents at nuclear power stations in other countries, causing severe health problems from radioactivity. The waste from nuclear power stations is also radioactive and will remain so for thousands of years. So there is a problem of storing nuclear waste.

Flight

Since the earliest days, people have looked up at the sky and imagined flying like birds. In the Greek legend, Icarus and his father made wings from feathers and wax, but Icarus flew too close to the sun, the wax melted, and he fell into the sea and drowned. In the real world, of course, they would not have been able to fly at all, because our arms are not strong enough for flight. In the natural world only birds, insects and some animals can fly. Birds use their wings to coast on warm, rising air currents. There are many different sizes and shapes of wings, and birds fly at different speeds.

Early attempts at flight

Inventors first attempted, around 400 BC, to copy the birds by making wings and strapping them to their arms. None of these attempts worked, however, so

people started to build machines to fly. They built gliders, which meant they could coast like birds on currents of air.

Balloon flight

The first recorded manned balloon flight in history was made in a hot air balloon built by the Montgolfier brothers on 21 November, 1783. The pilots, Jean-François Pilâtre de Rozier and Francois Laurent (the Marquis of d'Arlanders) flew for about 22 minutes.

Only a few days later Jacques Alexander Charles and Nicholas Louis Robert launched the first manned gas balloon. Again starting in Paris, the flight lasted over two hours and covered a distance of 56 km (25 miles).

When was the first commercial passenger service?

In 1914, between St Petersburg, Florida (USA) and Tampa, Florida (USA)

Who was the first woman to fly solo across the Atlantic?

Amelia Earhart (1897–1937) made a transatlantic solo flight in 1932.

Ballooning became fashionable and popular in the 18th century, and Ferdinand von Zeppelin made the first flight in a zeppelin (a type of airship) in 1900.

Aircraft

Aircraft are heavier than air but use thrust (forward motion created by the engine) to stay aloft. It was not until the start of the 20th century that heavier-than-air machines achieved flight. In 1903, the Wright brothers (Wilbur and Orville) built the first manned, power-driven, heavier-than-air flying machine. Their first flight was only 12 seconds long.

Acrobatic flying became popular, and newspapers offered large cash prizes for daredevil stunts. Long-distance flying also developed and an English newspaper sponsored a contest for the first flight across the English Channel. Louis Bleriot won this contest, flying from France to England in 1909 in a single wing plane. The first woman to gain a pilot's licence was Baroness Raymonde de la Roche (1884–1919), and the first aircraft to take off from water was flown by Henri Fabre (1882–1984).

Aircraft in wartime

The First World War was instrumental in the development of planes, from experiments to fully working machines. It was soon discovered that, to win the war, air control was vital. Aerial information, bombing and support provided valuable support to ground troops. World War I saw the birth of the fighter aircraft, or 'scouts', which still play a crucial role in modern history. The war also advanced bomber planes, so that they went from carrying only small bombs to deadly cargoes on purpose-built racks and housing.

In the 1930s both military and civil aircraft underwent a period of

development. Commercial air travel was an accepted form of transport. The first airliners were born, and they began crossing larger distances. More and more record-breaking flights were also being achieved. In 1927 Charles Lindbergh flew the first solo non-stop flight across the North Atlantic in his Ryan NYP monoplane, Spirit of St Louis.

Concorde

The Anglo-French machine Concorde was one of the world's greatest challenges in the history of aviation (flying). It cruised at more than twice the speed of sound at an altitude of 20,000 m (60,000 ft – eleven miles high). A typical flight from London to New York took fewer than four hours. Production of the plane ended in 1979, and all Concordes were withdrawn from service in 2000 after a crash near the Charles de Gaulle airport, Paris.

Helicopters

Helicopters were developed in the 20th century. The early designs were very unsuccessful, although some designs go back as far as the Renaissance artist and inventor Leonardo da Vinci's sketchbooks. Helicopters are used in war, to transport troops quickly, evacuate injured soldiers, and also to fight. In the civilian world, helicopters can be used as 'air ambulances' to reach injured people quickly, and get them to hospital.

Helicopters can land in quite remote and restricted places as they don't need a runway for landing or taking off as most aeroplanes do.

Food *and* farming

W e all know the importance of healthy eating to help keep us free from illness, and keep our bodies in good working condition. But do we know which foods to eat, and where they come from? Farming is an efficient way of growing the types of food people want to eat.

Five a day

To be strong and healthy, you need to eat lots of fruit and vegetables. This is important for good health, and can protect against illness. There are lots of fruit and vegetables which provide vital vitamins and fibre. Some of these can be grown in our own back gardens, such as carrots, broad beans, cucumbers, apples, gooseberries and rhubarb. Growing your own food helps to keep you active, and it's fun to do.

Dairy foods

As well as being one of the best sources of calcium, dairy products also provide protein, vitamins and minerals, and they're important for healthy bones and teeth. Milk and cheese are examples of dairy products. In Britain these foods come mainly from cows, sheep and goats.

Sustainable farming

Until early last century, all British farmers used sustainable methods, because they had little choice. Sustainable farming means growing food in ways that enable farmers to continue doing it. For example, traditional farmers depend on fossil fuels like oil for running their farm machines, on fertilisers to make plants grow better, and on pesticides to kill the insects that eat plants. When there's no oil left, how will farmers manage without tractors? What will they use instead of oil-based fertilisers?

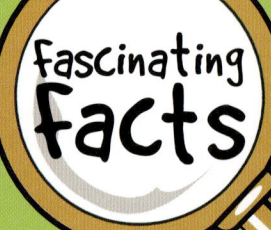

fascinating Facts

Lack of calcium (found in dairy products and leafy green vegetables) can prevent healthy bones forming.

A deficiency of vitamin A (from carrots and other highly coloured fruit and vegetables) can harm your eyesight.

Kiwi fruits contain nearly twice as much vitamin C as oranges.

Oily fish is essential for the development of the brain and nervous system, whilst eggs contain many nutrients which are crucial for healthy growth.

Organic farming

Organic farming is sustainable farming. It needs more workers and fewer machines, so more people will have farm jobs. And organic farming is said to be kinder to the land. But food produced by organic farming is more expensive than food produced by intensive farming.

Genetic engineering

Genetically modified (GM) crops are foods that have had a gene extracted from one plant, which has been placed into a different plant. GM crops are designed for many purposes, for example to produce a crop that stays fresh longer and to produce food with improved taste and quality.

GM plants could be kinder to the environment if they need fewer pesticides, fertilisers and water. Some people see GM technology as a way to help people in poor countries grow food.

Industrial farming

Industrial farming, also known as intensive agriculture, uses factory-type methods to produce large quantities of food. But in the long term, these methods may damage the land and pollute the air.

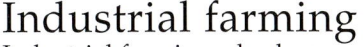

Are there risks with GM food?

Many people are suspicious of GM ingredients in food, as we don't know the risks that may be involved with eating these regularly.

Could GM farming be one solution to the problem of world hunger?

GM methods can increase production and lower the cost of food. They can be grown faster and cheaper, especially in areas suffering from drought.

Genetics

Genetics is the study of heredity, evolution and all life forms. Every human has similar characteristics, such as hair, legs and eyes, and genes are the instructions which make us all different, giving us blue or brown eyes, red or black hair. Genes are like the instructions that govern how every living creature looks and functions. The genetic information that makes us individual is inherited through chromosomes from our parents.

Each paired chromosome is composed of two tightly coiled strands of DNA (Deoxyribonucleic acid) that join in the middle to form an X shape. These strands of DNA have sections called genes, which contain the information that makes us unique. Unless you have an identical twin, your DNA is different from the DNA of every other person in the world, though it is the same in every cell in your body,

The vast majority of people have two copies of each gene, as we get one copy from each of our parents.

There is one copy of each gene on one of the pair of chromosomes we receive from our parents. As we receive two sets of instructions, this could cause confusion. But usually one gene is dominant: for example the gene for brown eyes is dominant over the gene for blue eyes (the gene for blue eyes is said to be recessive). In order to inherit blue eyes, a child must inherit two copies of the eye gene for blue eyes, one from each parent.

A momentous discovery

In 1953 two scientists, James D. Watson and Francis Crick, celebrated the fact that they had unravelled the structure of DNA. DNA is the material that makes up genes which pass hereditary characteristics from one parent to another. That momentous discovery was the culmination of research by scientists Maurice Wilkins and Rosalind Franklin. Powerful and controversial technologies are now available, including genetic engineering, stem cell research and DNA fingerprinting.

DNA fingerprinting

Each person's DNA is as unique as a fingerprint. Normal fingerprints occur only on the fingertips and can be altered by surgery. DNA 'fingerprints', however, can be taken even from bloodstained clothing and cannot be altered by any known treatment. Everyone has a different sequence of DNA. By identifying repeated patterns of DNA, scientists can identify whether DNA samples are from the same person, related people or people who are not related.

Can we clone dinosaurs?

We have only found a small proportion of the genetic information for dinosaurs so far. It is therefore not possible to clone a dinosaur at the moment, but it may be possible in the future.

What is DNA fingerprinting used for?

DNA fingerprinting can be used for anything from determining a biological mother or father to identifying the suspect of a crime.

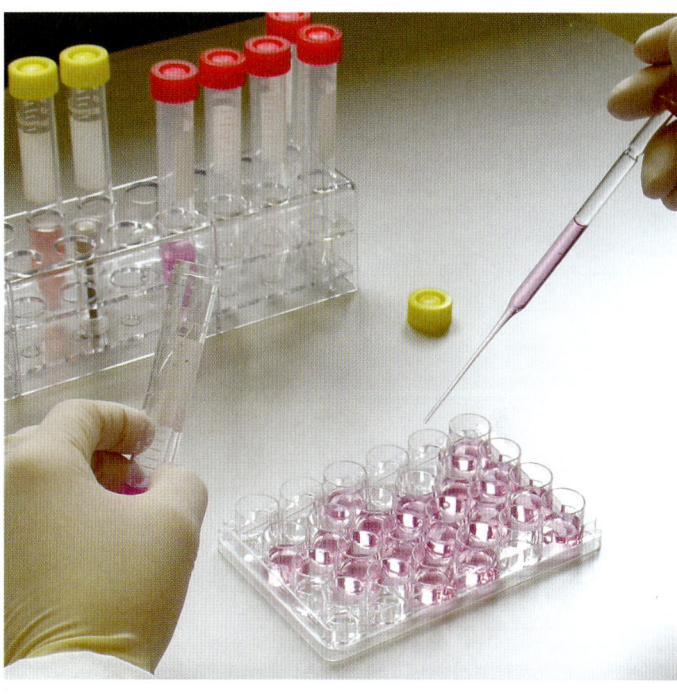

Stem cell research

Stem cells are cells that are present in the very early stages of an embryo's development. They can develop into any type of specialised cell. Stem cell research is investigating ways to produce cells to replace those damaged by diseases, such as Parkinson's Disease.

(breeding species with the same ancestors). A clone is any organism whose genetic information is identical to that of a 'mother organism' from which it was created. Some clones exist in nature; others are created by scientists. Dolly the sheep was the first mammal cloned from an adult cell.

Genetic engineering

Scientists are able to manipulate genes using genetic engineering. For years humans have been breeding animals and plants to get the characteristics they desire, for example, species that produce a lot of babies or new plants. Two techniques used to do this are selective breeding (breeding animals and plants by controlling the environment) and cross breeding

fascinating facts

James Watson, Francis Crick and Maurice Wilkins were awarded the Nobel Prize for their work in 1962. Rosalind Franklin died of cancer in April 1958, aged just 37, so never received a Nobel Prize for her crucial work in the discovery of DNA.

A giant model of a section of DNA, built from laboratory clamps and pieces of metal, is now in the Science Museum in London.

Global warming

M any scientists believe that gases in the air are causing the Earth's climate to gradually become hotter. This is called global warming.

Temperature and climate change

Measurements from the past 100 years show that the Earth's temperature has increased by 0.6°C (1°F). But scientists expect that over the next 100 years it will increase by an extra 1–3°C (2–6°F). This may not sound like much, but it could make the difference between life and death for some species on Earth, and dramatic changes to our climate!

What is the greenhouse effect?

In the Earth's atmosphere are tiny amounts of gases called 'greenhouse gases'. These gases let the sun's rays pass through to the Earth but hold in the heat that comes up from the sun-warmed Earth. This is called the 'greenhouse effect' – a natural process by which the Earth's atmosphere traps some of the sun's energy. It is this warmth that allows the Earth to support life – just as a greenhouse in your garden traps heat to keep growing plants warm enough.

A natural process gone wrong

Most scientists believe humans are now creating too many greenhouse gases, unnaturally increasing the greenhouse effect. When too many greenhouse gases are added to the atmosphere, the 'walls' of our greenhouse (the 'thermal blanket') get thicker. More heat gets trapped in the atmosphere and the temperature of the Earth goes up. A process that has been beneficial to life on Earth becomes potentially harmful.

What is causing global warming?

• Burning fossils fuels such as coal releases carbon dioxide, one of the greenhouse gases that contributes to global warming.

• Deforestation – cutting or burning down huge areas of the world's forests which increases the carbon dioxide in the atmosphere. This is because trees and other plants

The last Ice Age was a mere 7°F colder than today. That's a little less than 4°C!

The six hottest recorded years in history were all in the 1990s.

'breathe in' carbon dioxide and 'breathe out' oxygen, thus helping to lower the amounts of carbon dioxide in our air.
• As rubbish decays, another harmful greenhouse gas called methane is released into the atmosphere.

Q&A?

How long have we known about the greenhouse effect?

The French scientist Joseph Fourier first wrote about this in 1824, though he didn't call it the greenhouse effect.

Possible consequences of global warming

Melting ice Ice covers 3% of the Earth's surface and is the world's largest supply of fresh water. Warmer weather causes glaciers (huge, slow-moving sheets of ice) – and even the polar ice caps – to melt. Many of our glaciers are already melting.

Rising seas Melting glaciers add water to the ocean. Rising sea levels would mean coastal flooding and could cause salt water to flow into areas where salt would harm plants and animals.

Droughts and diseases Cold places on the Earth may become warmer, and this could mean a chance to plant crops in places that were formerly too cold.

However, areas that already have hot climates might become too hot, bringing drought and leaving people without enough to eat. Tropical diseases like malaria might become more common in newly warmed areas.

Extreme weather A warmer world is expected to experience more extreme weather – more rain during wet times, more powerful storms and longer periods of drought.

What can we do?

There are many things people can do to help stop global warming. These are just some of them:
• **Save electricity** Use low-energy light bulbs and switch things off when they are not needed.
• **Reduce car use** Walk, cycle or take the bus.

• **Recycle** Plastic bags, cans, newspapers and many other items can be recycled, so that less rubbish goes to landfill sites. Buy recyclable products instead of non-recyclable ones.
• **Reuse** Even better than recycling is using things again. Buy things that have less packaging and create less waste.
• **Choose items carefully** Some cars are better for the environment than others because they can travel longer on a smaller amount of fuel.
• **Plant trees** Trees absorb carbon dioxide from the air.

Gravity

Force is the pressure used when something is pushed or pulled. Forces are all round us. When you throw a ball in the air, it is pulled back to the ground by gravity. Gravity is a natural force that pulls objects on or near the Earth's surface towards its centre. In other words, it keeps us all fixed to the surface of the earth.

Gravity keeps the moon going round the Earth, the Earth going round the sun, and the sun going round the centre of the Milky Way. It's the force that governs motion in the universe.

Objects with mass (a measure of weight) attract each other, no matter how small or large they are. The strength of attraction depends on the weight of the objects and the distance between them.

In orbit

An object remains in orbit around a mass, such as a planet, due to that planet's gravity. For instance, the Earth is surrounded by it's own gravitational field, and so objects in orbit around the Earth are attracted to the Earth and therefore maintain their orbit.

Are clouds affected by gravity?

No, because clouds are made of very small particles of ice and water and are too light, and so they just float. However, they can combine together and form rain drops The rain drops are much bigger and so gravity pulls them down.

Is gravity the same everywhere?

Gravity at the equator is slightly less than at the North Pole, because the Earth bulges at the equator and you are further from the centre of the Earth.

Isaac Newton (1643–1727)

He was the first person to study gravity seriously, and he had the insight to realise that the force that holds us to the Earth is the same one that keeps the planets in their orbits around the sun. He worked out the mathematical nature of the mutual (two-way) force, and he correctly argued that gravity acts across the entire universe.

Newton had read Galileo and Johannes Kepler's work on how planets circle the sun and how things fall to the Earth. Galileo (1564–1642) was an Italian physicist, astronomer and philosopher. Kepler (1571–1630) was a German mathematician, astronomer and astrologer. He wondered whether the force that kept the moon from being thrown away from the Earth could explain gravity on the Earth's surface. Newton made this link in 1666, and called his findings the Law of Universal Gravitation. There is a famous story that Newton made the connection between the two ideas because of an apple falling in an orchard. However, it is more likely that the idea did not come to him in a flash of inspiration, but was developed over time.

Albert Einstein

Newton's description remained unchanged until Albert Einstein published his General Theory of Relativity in 1915. Einstein modified Newton's view of gravity by arguing that the gravitational force is a sign of the curvature of space-time. Although Einstein's idea is necessary for describing the evolution of the universe as a whole, Newton's theory works well enough when gravitational forces are not very strong.

You can read more about Albert Einstein on pages 6–7.

The human body *and* health

The human body is made up of bones, muscles, internal organs and skin. The bones act like a frame. Muscles are attached to bones and make it possible to move. Internal organs are responsible for the functions that keep us alive. The brain controls these and, together with the central nervous system allows us to be aware of what is happening around us. Skin is an organ that covers the whole of the body, protecting it, and preventing it from drying out.

The brain

The brain works like a central computer monitoring what is happening outside and continually monitoring and adjusting what is happening inside. The brain ensures that body temperature is kept constant and that there is enough oxygen and glucose in the blood.

The digestive and respiratory systems

All parts of the body need a mixture of oxygen and glucose (energy). The digestive and respiratory systems provide these. The digestive system is made up of the mouth, the gullet, the stomach, and the small and large intestines. Food taken in through the mouth is broken down and the energy that it contains is absorbed. The waste products remaining eventually form faeces in the bowel. The respiratory system is made up of the nose and lungs. As we breathe oxygen is taken in and carbon dioxide is exhaled.

Oxygen and energy

Oxygen and energy are moved round the body by the circulatory system, which is made up of the heart and blood vessels. Blood is kept flowing through the circulatory system by the pumping action of the heart. Oxygen and energy are taken to muscles and carbon dioxide and other waste products are carried away. Carbon dioxide is taken to the lungs where it is breathed out. Other waste products are taken to the liver and kidneys. These organs filter the blood, removing waste products. Waste products removed by the kidneys go into the urine and some of those removed by the liver go into the large intestine. Urine collects in the bladder, which is emptied periodically.

What is the largest organ in the body?

The skin.

How many times will the human heart beat in an average lifetime?

Your heart beats about 100,000 times in one day and about 35,000,000 times in a year. That's 2,800,000,000 times in an average lifetime!

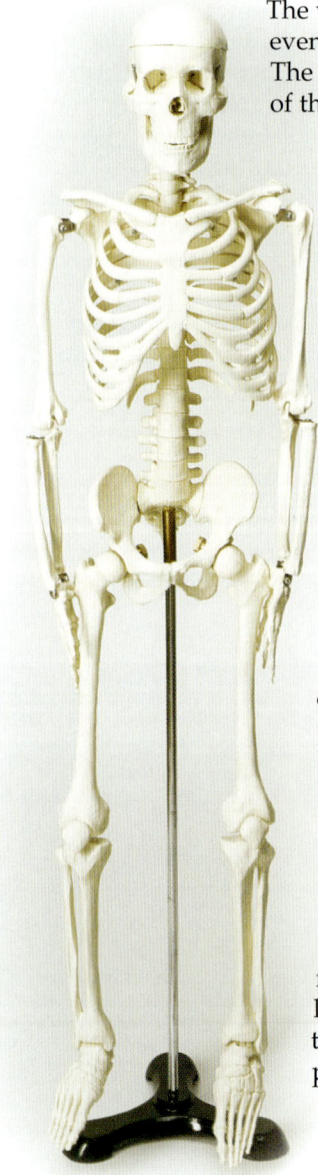

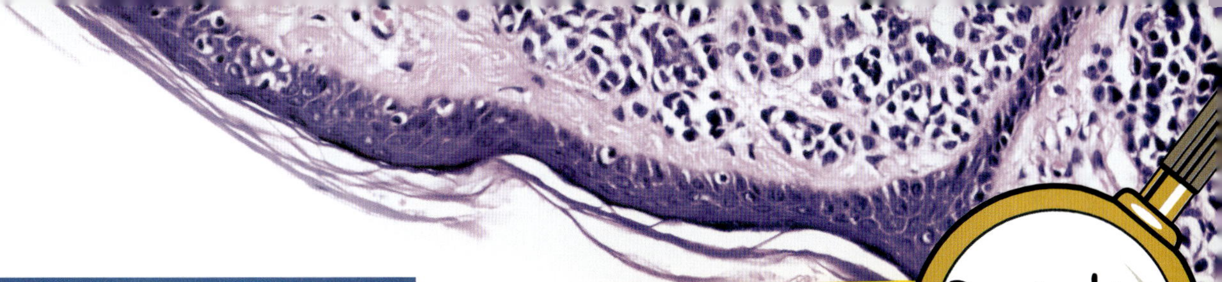

Every 30 days we have a completely new skin.

There are more than 200 different bones in the human body.

The small intestine is 5 metres long.

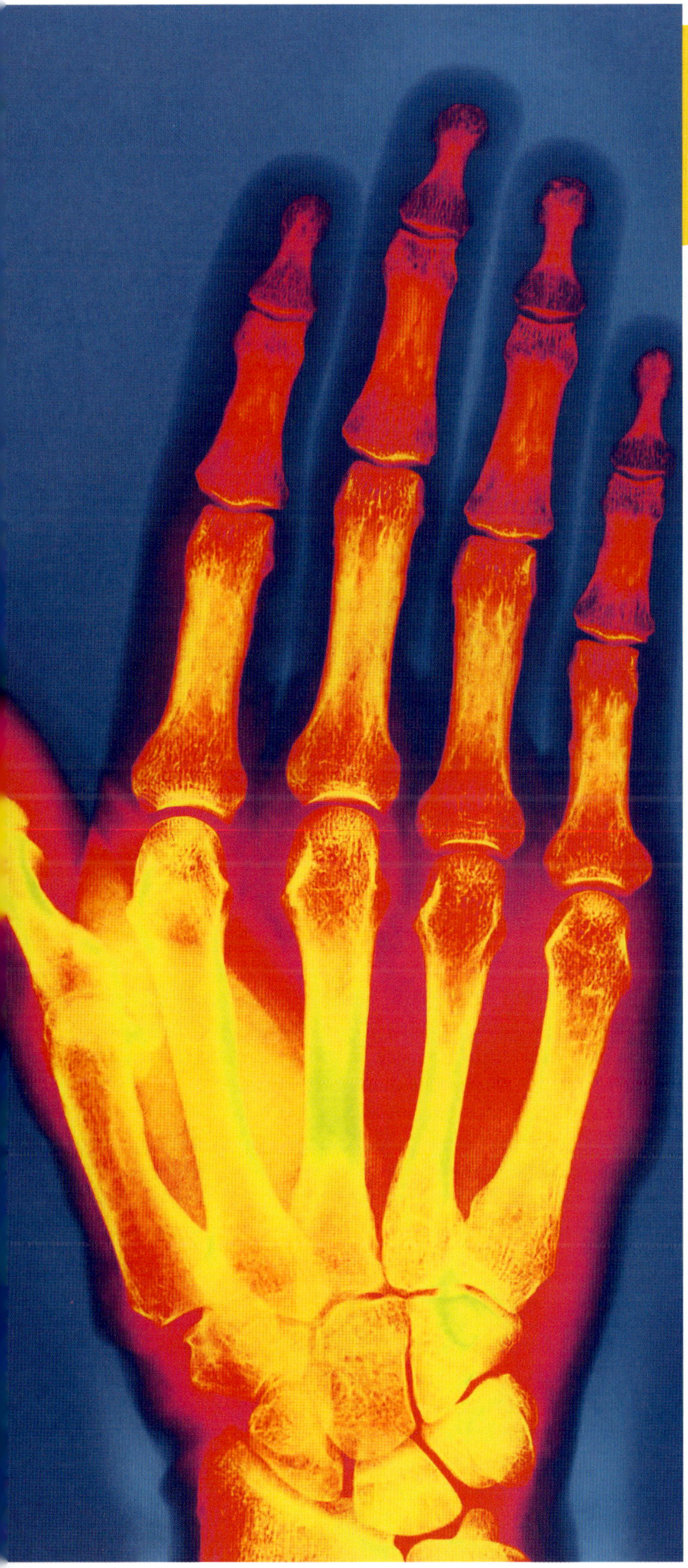

The senses

The senses are the way in which we know about the world around us – they are sight, hearing, smell, taste and touch.

Eyes are designed much like a camera. Light enters through the pupil, and is focused by the lens on the retina – the light-sensitive surface at the back of the eye. This information goes to the brain.

There are two parts to the ear: the outer ear (the part we can see) and the ear canal – a tube that goes into the head. In the middle ear is the eardrum. Sound waves make the eardrum vibrate and the vibrations are passed along three tiny bones to the inner ear (cochlea) which converts the movements into information that the brain interprets as sound.

The sense of smell depends on a collection of cells at the back of the nose, that are sensitive to minute quantities of chemicals, for example those given off by freshly baked bread.

The 'taste' of something is really a combination of smell and taste. When we eat or drink the tongue detects the basic tastes – sweet, sour, bitter and salty, and we also smell it. The brain puts both together and comes up with the overall taste.

Touch is different from the other senses because we have a sense of touch all over the body. Nerve endings in the skin can detect cold, heat, pain and pressure. Together these make up the sense of touch.

Keeping the body healthy

Keeping the body healthy involves:

- Eating a balanced diet to ensure that you have enough energy for activity and enough nutrients to grow and repair.
- Taking regular exercise to keep the muscles strong and the lungs clear.
- Getting enough sleep.
- Not smoking cigarettes because they contain chemicals that do long term damage to the lungs, heart and blood vessels.

Magnetism

M agnetism is the force which pulls objects made of metal such as iron, nickel or cobalt towards a magnet. A magnet creates a magnetic field (an area in which a magnetic force can be felt).

Dynamos and motors

A changing or moving electrical charge generates a magnetic field; similarly if an electrical conductor such as a length of wire is moved through a magnetic field then an electrical current is created in it. This effect was first discovered by Michael Faraday in 1831 and is at the core of almost every electrical generator – a loop or coil of wire is rotated inside a permanent magnet, and as the coil moves through the magnetic field an electrical current is created inside the wire. Devices like this are called dynamos.

This same relationship between magnetic field, current and motion is used in the electric motor. As with a dynamo a coil or loop of wire is positioned within a permanent magnet. However, rather than moving the coil to generate electrical current an electrical current is passed through the coil and generates motion – the coil rotates!

fascinating **Facts**

If you take a magnet and repeatedly rub it from the top to the bottom of an iron nail you will find that the nail becomes magnetised.

Take an ordinary magnet, put it under a piece of paper, sprinkle iron filings over the paper. See the way the filings align themselves to the field of the magnet!

All materials contain tiny particles called electrons. These electrons have an electrical charge and spin around. As they do this they generate tiny magnetic fields. In most materials these tiny magnetic fields all point in different directions so overall they cancel out – but in some materials these tiny fields can be aligned by stroking with a magnet so that they point in the same direction. These materials are said to be magnetic – iron is an example of a magnetic material.

Even in a magnetic material like iron not all the little magnetic fields are pointing in the same direction, instead you get lots of regions – within each region the magnetic fields are all aligned but the different regions are still pointing in different directions. This means the material's overall magnetic field is still pretty small. However if a magnetic material like this is placed in another magnetic field all the regions will tend to align to point in the

same direction as this field – so they all end up pointing in the same direction and the material then gets its own net magnetic field too!

The Earth is a magnet!

Electrical currents in the liquid iron at the core of the Earth create their own magnetic field, closely aligned to the axis around which the Earth rotates. This magnetic field is how compasses work and how we navigate. Take a magnet and suspend it so it's free to rotate, then the magnet will settle so that it's aligned with the Earth's magnetic field. This means it will be pointing almost North–South. The magnetic north is nearly but not quite at the same place as the geographic North Pole.

Navigating by magnetism

Humans are not the only creatures to use the Earth's magnetic field to find their way about. Recent studies have shown that many creatures, from bacteria to whales, can sense the Earth's magnetic field and use this information to navigate. Loggerhead sea turtles, for instance, can sense the intensity and direction of the Earth's magnetic field and use this to navigate their 13,000 km (8,078 miles) migration around the Atlantic Ocean.

How do magnets attract iron and other magnetic materials?

When the magnet is brought close to the magnetic material, the fields in the material align with the magnet and 'pull' the material towards it.

What are the Northern Lights?

The Aurora Borealis or Northern Lights are produced when charged particles trapped in the Earth's magnetic field are released into the atmosphere causing some gases to give off light in 'curtains' and 'ribbons'.

Medicine *and* disease

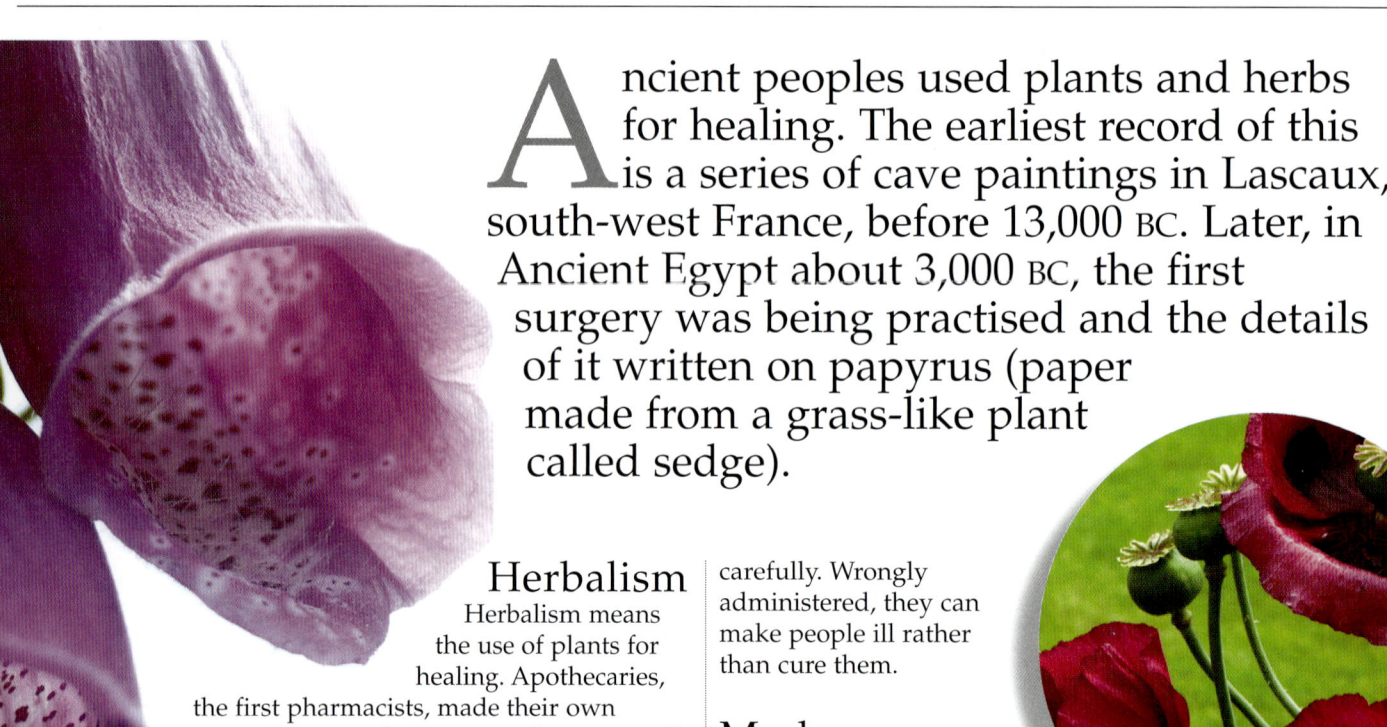

Ancient peoples used plants and herbs for healing. The earliest record of this is a series of cave paintings in Lascaux, south-west France, before 13,000 BC. Later, in Ancient Egypt about 3,000 BC, the first surgery was being practised and the details of it written on papyrus (paper made from a grass-like plant called sedge).

Herbalism

Herbalism means the use of plants for healing. Apothecaries, the first pharmacists, made their own medicines and ointments. Plants are still widely used today, for medicines and in traditional remedies. Morphine and codeine (from the opium poppy, right) and aspirin (from the willow tree) are used as painkillers. Digitalis from the foxglove (left) is used to treat heart conditions, while quinine from the bark of the cinchona tree has long been used to combat malaria.

However, even though plants are natural they must be used very carefully. Wrongly administered, they can make people ill rather than cure them.

Modern medicine

Many discoveries and inventions in the 19th century have created great advances in medicine which are still important today. The death rate of new mothers was dramatically cut after 1847, when Ignaz Semmelweis experimented with doctors using soap to wash their hands. This was followed by Joseph Lister's experiments leading to the invention of antiseptics in 1865. Meanwhile Louis Pasteur linked micro-organisms with disease, making a great advance in medical thinking. In preventive health care, Pasteur also made the first anti-rabies

Why is children's medicine called paediatrics?

The word paediatrics is derived from two Greek words, paidi which means 'boy' and 'iatros' which means 'doctor'.

Who invented the sticking plaster?

The adhesive plaster was invented in 1920 by Earle Dickson, who was a cotton buyer for a company that made bandages. He invented the sticking plaster because it was easy to use – his wife had lots of kitchen accidents!

vaccine in 1885 and invented pasteurisation of milk, helping to limit the spread of disease. In the late 1880s Robert Koch made the first important discoveries in bacteriology.

The combination of 19th century medical discoveries and inventions and improved living conditions led to higher life expectancy, and a significant reduction in disease, for people in many parts of the world. Further developments in the 20th century have led to vastly improved levels of health around the world, and higher expectations of health.

Specialist areas of modern medicine:

Dermatology	treatment of skin conditions
Neurology	dealing with the brain and nervous system
Oncology	treatment of cancer
Ophthalmology	treating eyes
Orthopaedics	treatment of the spine and other bones
Paediatrics	children's medicine
Psychiatry	dealing with mental illness
Surgery	invasive treatments, which 'enter' the body

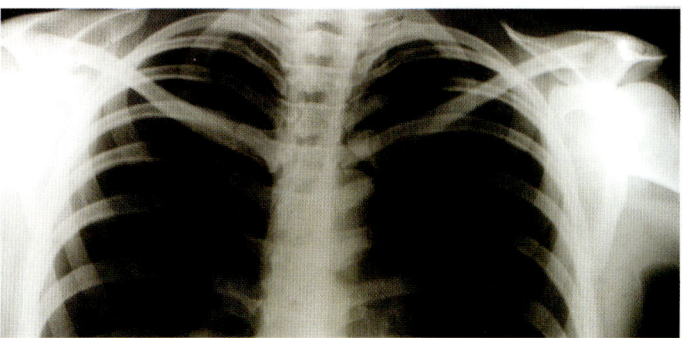

X-ray of human chest

Timeline of medical inventions

1280	spectacles (glasses)
1540	artificial limbs
1714	the mercury thermometer
1792	the ambulance
1796	vaccination
1816	the stethoscope
1846	anaesthesia
1853	the syringe
1865	antiseptic treatments
1885	anti-rabies vaccination
1887	contact lenses
1895	X-rays
1928	antibiotics
1967	heart transplant
1979	ultrasound

Garlic

Fascinating Facts

Garlic was given to Roman legionnaires at Hadrian's Wall to help them fight off colds and flu in the bitter English winter.

Hippocrates of Cos (460 BC – 370 BC) was an ancient Greek physician who is commonly regarded as one of the most outstanding figures in the history of medicine. He gives his name to the 'Hippocratic Oath' which is taken by all doctors.

Natural resources

Many countries use coal, oil and gas for their energy. These are called 'fossil fuels' because they have been formed from the remains of prehistoric plants and animals. However, they are 'non-renewable', meaning they cannot be renewed or replaced. Coal and oil will eventually run out, or become too expensive to take from the ground. But some energy sources are renewable – they never run out. The sun provides renewable energy, because it shines every day. Wind energy is also renewable: the wind stops blowing – but it always starts again!

Fossil fuels like coal and oil provide about two-thirds of the world's electricity and 95% of the world's total energy, including heating and transport. Coal is used in power stations to generate (produce) a lot of electricity, quite cheaply. Also, transporting the coal to the power stations is easy. So, power stations (which make electricity) use coal, oil or gas because they are very efficient fuels.

Pollution

The main disadvantage of fossil fuels is pollution. Burning coal or oil produces carbon dioxide, which contributes to the 'greenhouse effect', warming the Earth. Secondly, burning fossil fuels produces sulphur dioxide, a gas that causes acid rain which damages plants. Thirdly, mining (digging up) coal can ruin and destroy large areas of the landscape, and spoil the beauty of the countryside.

Non-renewable resources

Once we've burned all the coal, oil and gas, there isn't any more. Our consumption of fossil fuels has nearly doubled every 20 years since 1900. This is a particular problem for oil, because we use it to make plastic and many other products.

Renewable energy

In addition to the sun and the wind, there are several sources of renewable energy: plants, the Earth and the oceans.

Sun and wind

Sunlight, or solar energy, can be used directly for heating and lighting homes and offices, for generating electricity, and for heating water. Solar power can also be used in factories.

Hydropower

Falling water can be used to drive a turbine – a spinning machine which makes electricity. This is called hydropower (hydro and water). Waterfalls can be used to make hydropower. Sometimes an existing waterfall is used, or a dam can be built on a river to make a new waterfall.

Biomass

The living material in plants is called biomass. Biomass can be used to produce electricity, chemicals or fuel for cars. For example, the oil in some plants can be used to make a kind of petrol.

How can waves be used to make electricity?

The tides and the winds drive the waves. The oceans move forward and back, following a regular pattern. The energy of the tides can be captured by special machines.

What is geothermal energy?

The inside of the Earth is very hot. Geothermal energy uses the Earth's internal heat for various uses. This energy from the Earth can be used to heat buildings or make electricity.

Fascinating Facts

The average household throws away almost 8.5 kg (19 lb) of paper each week. Most types of paper can be recycled; the more paper we recycle the fewer trees need to be cut down – because paper is made from pulped trees!

Hydrogen is the most abundant element on the Earth. It can be burned as a fuel, or converted into electricity.

The solar system

The sun, the centre of our solar system, is a giant, spinning ball of very hot gas. The light from the sun heats our world and makes life possible. The solar system consists of the sun and nine planets (and their moons) which orbit the sun. Scientists study the planets and stars with very sophisticated equipment, such as radio telescopes and satellites.

A satellite

The planets

The inner planets (those planets that orbit close to the sun) are quite different from the outer planets (those planets that orbit far away from the sun).

The inner planets
Mercury, Venus, Earth and Mars are the inner planets. They are relatively small, composed mostly of rock, and have few or no moons.

Mercury is the closest planet to the sun and is the fastest-moving planet. Temperatures on Mercury range between 400°C and –170°C (750°F and –274°F).

Venus is a similar size to the Earth; it is the brightest and, at 475°C (887°F), the hottest of the planets, due to its atmosphere of carbon dioxide gas which traps the sun's energy. Scientists have tried to send probes onto this scorching planet, but the atmosphere has proved too hot.

Earth looks blue and white from space due to the oceans and clouds which cover its surface. It consists of a solid crust above a molten layer, at the centre of which is a solid iron core. Earth is surrounded by a layer of gases which form an atmosphere, and 71% of its surface is covered with liquid water – a property unique in the Solar System and which has enabled life to develop. The Earth is 152 million km (94.5 million miles) from the sun.

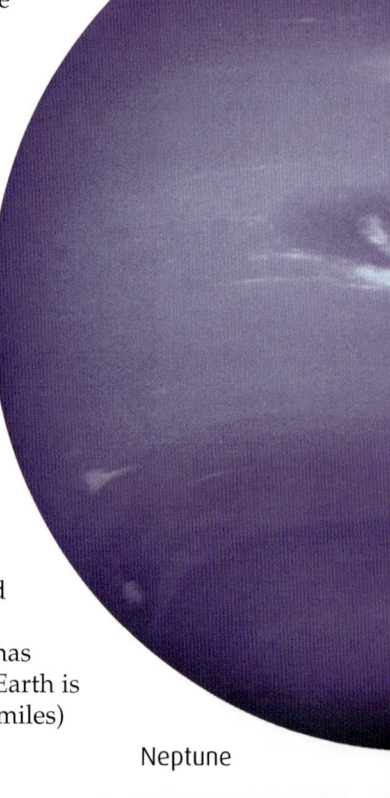

Neptune

Mars also has an atmosphere and has, in the past, had water, leading to theories that there might be life on Mars. Space probes have tested the surface and found no trace of life.

The outer planets are Jupiter, Saturn, Uranus, Neptune and Pluto. They are mostly very large, mostly gaseous, ringed and have many moons. Pluto is the exception – it is small, rocky and has one moon.

The largest planet, Jupiter, consists of hydrogen and helium and is covered by clouds.

Saturn is famous for its rings, which are 270,000 km (167,000 miles) across but only 200 m (660 ft) thick. The rings are made of chunks of ice varying from snowball to iceberg size.

Uranus is a very cold planet, as it is 20 times further from the heat of the sun than the Earth.

Very little was known about Neptune until the Voyager 2 spacecraft showed pictures of its blue-green clouds.

Pluto is the smallest, coldest and most distant planet in the Solar System. It was only discovered in 1930. Surface temperatures are –233°C (–387.5°F).

Stars

A star is an enormous ball of gas. It generates energy and therefore emits light. All stars except the sun appear as tiny shining points

Is the moon a planet?

No. The moon is Earth's natural satellite. It is a cold, dry orb whose surface is covered with craters and scattered with rocks and dust. The moon has no atmosphere. It is possible that there is some frozen ice on the moon.

Do stars last forever?

The average life span of a yellow star, like the sun, is about 10 billion years. The sun will eventually burn out in about 5 to 6 billion years.

in the night sky that twinkle because of the effect of the Earth's atmosphere and their distance from us. The sun is also a star and although only a medium-sized one, it is close enough to Earth to appear as a disk and to provide daylight.

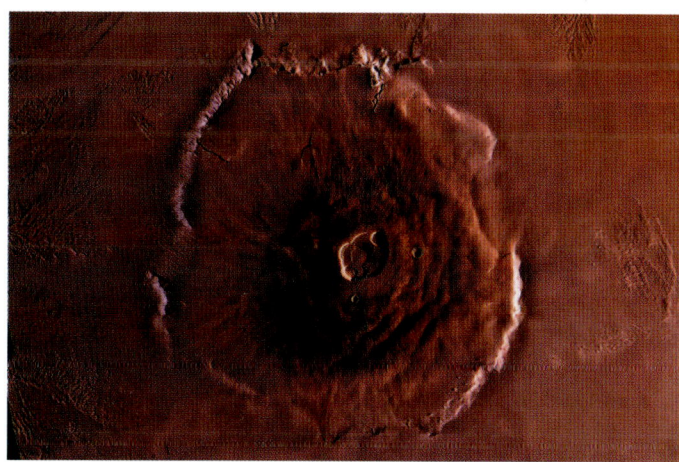

Olympus Mons

Fascinating Facts

Viewed edge-on, Saturn's rings seem to disappear. Jupiter, Uranus and Neptune also have rings, but these are much fainter.

Mars is the home of Olympus Mons, the largest volcano found in the solar system. It stands about 27 km (17 miles) high with a crater 50 miles (81 km) wide.

The solar system

Water

W ater has the chemical formula H_2O, which means each water molecule is made of two hydrogen atoms and one oxygen atom. Water is the only substance that naturally occurs in solid, liquid and gaseous forms on the Earth.

Water is very important to life. Roughly 97% of the Earth's water is held in the oceans, which cover approximately 70% of the Earth's surface.

How is water vapour important?

Water vapour in the atmosphere is a greenhouse gas – it helps to reduce the amount of heat escaping from the planet into space. If there were no water vapour in the atmosphere the average temperature on the Earth would be –18°C (0.4°F)!

How are polar ice caps important?

The polar ice caps are extremely important to the global climate. They reflect heat more efficiently than the oceans or land and so help to regulate the amount of heat the Earth absorbs from the sun. They also lock away vast quantities of water that would otherwise be part of the oceans – if all the ice in the world were to melt the average sea level would rise by 70 m (230 ft)!

Water has the following physical properties:
- Its freezing point is 0°C (32°F) and its boiling point is 100°C (212°F).
- A litre of water weighs 1 kg (2.2 lbs).
- Its pH is 7, meaning it is neutral (see Acids and alkalis, page 12 for more on this).
- It is an excellent solvent, meaning lots of things, particularly salts, will dissolve very well in it.
- It absorbs more red light (and infra-red) than blue light, so large bodies of pure water appear blue.